MAY DREAMS.

BY

HENRY L. ABBEY.

Des lebens Mai blüht einmal, und nicht wieder.—SCHILLER.

NEW YORK:
ABBEY & ABBOT, PUBLISHERS,
119 NASSAU ST.
M DCCC LXII.

Entered, according to Act of Congress, in the year 1862, by Abbey & Abbot, In the Clerk's Office of the District Court of the United States, for the Southern District of New York.

STEREOTYPED AND PRINTED BY
F. SOMERS, 13 SPRUCE STREET, N. Y.

TO

WILLIAM CULLEN BRYANT.

CONTENTS.

MAY DREAMS.

MAY DREAMS.

O May! robed in your gown of flowers,
  Nun-like, gaze from your balmy cell,
  Under your crown of asphodel,
And sentinel all the summer hours;
Rising among your daisy bowers,
  Like Venus from her cradled shell!

O May! your cheeks are sunset skies,
  Which the lips of the verge shall press,
  And the amber clouds caress—
Drifting along in the light which lies
Over your soul-lit, jasmine eyes,
  In all its golden tenderness!

O May! you seem a silver sea,
  Glassing an earthly, ether dome;
  For the songs of the robins come,
Like the dashing of waves to me,
Whose waters the sunlight seems to be,
  And the lilies, the downy foam.

O May! fountain of dulcet days,
  And nature's vernal blossoming
  Of woodland haunts, where pansies cling
With blue-bells, round untrodden ways,
From your dreamy, crystalline rays
  Riseth the fairy sylph of Spring!

O May! you seem a tinted shell,
  Upon a tropical, flowret shore
  Dashed by the waves of zephyrs o'er—
A conch, wherein the sink and swell
Of soundless symphonies, float and dwell,
  Heard in the heart forevermore.

Down sinuous paths I tread, and turn
  By dells where insects, in their flight,
  Seem like stars in a silver night;
Where flowers are but the words I learn,
Through means which we cannot discern,
  Set to the music of the light.

Here, alone, I can once more be
  One with the hills, the rocks and trees,
  And wrap my being up in these,
In a mystic eternity;
Feeling more than I know or see,
  Lost in immortal fantasies.

Here in a realm of wordless dreams—
  That inner life which knows and thinks;
  My thirsty spirit comes and drinks
The petal dew of golden streams;
Where death is less than what it seems,
  And life is subtler than the Sphinx.

I wander through the sylvan vales,
  Lush with the richness of the day,
  Where each crocus, in pied array,
Over the leaves of grass prevails ;
Like boats on a dark green sea, whose sails
  Float in the balmy breath of May.

Here the marigold, dipped in sheen,
  In nooks of quiet, ripe and rare,
  Swayeth its beauties fresh and fair,
Above the dewy bank of green ;
And seems a fairy palace, seen
  Lit up, and drifting in the air.

Thoughts of the loved and lost arise,
  The shadow presence comes again,
  I feel once more my balm of pain,
I see the moonlight of dear eyes ;
And all that in the past I prize,
  Falls on my dreams like tender rain.

I see the tulips in the glade,
  Filled with the incense of the day,
  Like tiny censers swing and sway
Before an altar formed of shade ;
Where crickets, in the grass arrayed,
  Shall pipe the matin mass of May.

I see the mountains rimmed with gold,
  The verdant meadows veined with rills ;
  And aura, which the light distills,
Float far along the distant wold,
And o'er the waterfall, unrolled
  Like some bright banner 'gainst the hills.

But vain were all of these to me,
  Had I no golden memories here :
  In other eyes these scenes were dear ;
The purling stream, the emerald lea,
Recall some cherished phantasy,
  And joys departed, re-appear.

And so,in forest lawns and lanes,
  Where mid the friths of fern I stray,
  I dream the saddened hours away ;
But yet some mourning fancy reigns,
And to the vernal view complains,
  O, would that life might be all May !

The years like birds of passage go
  To that eternal clime, the past ;
  And May's immortal lot is cast
Upon their flight o'er all below,
Like sunlight on a field of snow,
  Or some sweet rose-leaf on the blast.

The hours their joys and sorrows bring,
  Bright Summer makes the hills sublime,
  Ripe Autumn bears its frosty rime,
And Winter crowns the north wind king ;
But May is but a crystal spring,
  That empties in the tide of time.

SHIPS AT SEA.

HAVE you stood upon the coast
        Of the sea?
Looking out upon the host,
        On the sea,
Of the ships, which, here and there,
Seem like cloudlets in the air,
Yet bring burdens rich and rare
        O'er the sea?

How the evanescent light
        Paints the sails!

Casting back a lustre bright,
    From the sails,
'Till it shimmers high and low,
And it pictures in its glow,
Shadows, in the deep below,
    Of the sails!

How the ships go sailing round
    O'er the sea!
'Till the destined coast is found
    O'er the sea!
Yet when bitter storms arise—
Eyelids drooping o'er the skies—
Many a ship dismantled lies
    On the sea.

So upon the sea of life
    There are wrecks—
Surging wildly in the strife
    Human wrecks!
Shattered by the furious waves,

Where the storm of passion raves,
Whelming, in its yawning graves,
Helpless wrecks.

Poets thoughts are ships at sea,
In his brain—
Sailing wildly o'er the sea
Of his brain;
And the argosies come in
To the harbor of his pen,
With the fire, Promethean,
Of the brain.

Many are the ships at sea,
In the mind—
Drifting round upon the sea
Of the mind—
Ships of Love and Hate and Fear—
Ships of Sorrow, dark and drear,
Sailing 'mid the tempests sear
Of the mind.

Human hearts are ships at sea,
    Drifting round—
Hearts—thy type eternity!
    Drifting round—
Drifting, ever drifting o'er
That bright sea whose either shore
Is the land where evermore
    Peace is found.

O, I love the dancing sea
    With its sails!
And I gaze in ecstasy
    On the sails
Of the ships, which here and there
Seem like cloudlets in the air;
Yet are bringing burdens rare
    With their sails.

LEAH.

THE Summer-time will come again
  To kiss the brow of dying Spring,
And, with the south wind's low refrain,
  A choral requiem will she sing.
The valley and the everglade
  Will bloom again, perchance as now,
By many a modest flower arrayed—
    But, Leah, where art thou?

The pansies peeping from the grass,
  By zephyrs may be rocked to dreams,
And floods of sunshine, as they pass,
  Will bathe them in their golden beams.
The long, bright tresses of the day,
  Shall cluster brighter round its brow,

And waft them, lotus-like, away—
    But, Leah, where art thou?

The moon will press her dimpled cheek
  Against the bosom of the sky,
And, as we dreamed once, seem to speak
  To silver clouds which drift them by.
Like men before the upraised Host,
  The wavy grass again will bow
Before the breeze it loveth most—
    But, Leah, where art thou?

Again the cloak-like clouds will fall,
  And wrap them round the mountain's base,
Leaving their peaks, so gaunt and tall,
  Like islands in the sea of space—
That ether sea, whose phantom waves
  Dash heaven's shores—as thoughts, a brow—
Where beauty never sinks in graves—
    But, Leah, where art thou?

And so I sit and muse, and dream
  On fancies shimmering bright and free ;
For each one is a crystal stream
  Which ever tends its course to thee—
To thee, loved Leah. In my heart
  There is a void which echoes now,
'Till that sad question seems its part—
    Dear Leah, where art thou?

And now the days will come and go
  Like shadows on a mountain stream :
And I will bow me down in woe,
  And mourn thee, bright, departed dream.
The Summer-time will come again,
  And flowers will cling them round her brow,
Like memory-pictures round the brain—
    But, Leah, where art thou?

QUEEN AZORE.

My loved and beautiful bride, Azore,
  Stooped to drink at the wayside spring,
When, riding up from the crescent shore,
  Garbed as a hunter, came the King.
He begged, with a smile, to quaff the bowl,
  But still his heart to her eyes would cling—
Those sea-blue boundaries of her soul.

A cry went out o'er the land for war—
  You who have heard it know how it thrills!
I dreamed that this was my rising star,
  So in the breath of the daffodils,

Which sails the blowing tamarisks o'er
  To the impervious haze of hills,
I bade adieu to my bride Azore.

Pointing to cliffs in the wilderness,
  I said, ere weeping I turned away:
Lo! the years their saddened lips shall press
  And leave their traces in slow decay
On these, but not on my love for thee.
  Then the clouds loomed up across the day,
Like bergs of ice from the Northern Sea.

So, for the rights and the hopes of man,
  'Mid serried rank, and weary, and sore,
I marched far north with the army's van,
  To pitch our tents on an alien shore.
Then, with iron lips and flaming breath,
  The booming shock of the battle ran
Along the lines, from the gorge of death.

Then it chanced that men unfurled my fame,
  Like a rare gonfalon to the air ;
And oft while I dreamed, a vision came
  And rose o'er the bastion's scaling stair,
And the grim guns on the parapet o'er—
  A sweet, vague vision, white-robed and fair :
My fair and lovable bride Azore.

I closed my eyes in a blissful gloom,
  While sated with rose blows down the gale :
A voice is borne on the rich perfume,
  Up from the platanes of the vale.
As I seek for her who calls aloud,
  Above the meshes of fragrant bloom,
In cornice of darkness hangs a cloud.

So, with a nameless feeling of loss,
  I took the way for my home once more,
When peace, like a great, white Albatross,
  Passed over the realm from shore to shore.

The King gave honors that might be seen—
  Gave me the hand of the bride Azore :
My bride no more, but Azore the Queen !

'Tis the same old story o'er again,
  Of broken vows and a blighted trust—
Of two hearts severed in wrong and pain—
  I murmur ! yet all God's ways are just.
For a watchful sense this record keeps—
  My love for the Queen is trailed in dust,
But honor sits in her heart and weeps.

ON THE RONDOUT.

Brightly each glowing moonbeam falls
  Upon thy cheek, O beauteous stream!
While Naiads, from their wat'ry halls,
  Come up to drink the midnight dream;
And, peeping forth their sparkling eyes—
  Glist'ning like amethystine dew—
They cause the tiny swells which rise,
  To seem like stars reflected through.

As in this drifting bark I sit,
  And float me slowly down the tide—
Watching the shadows, as they flit
  From off the shores on either side—

I picture, in my fancy free,
  An old, old story o'er again;
But rustling zephyrs, wafting me,
  Bear off the mem'ry from my brain.

High loom the hills on either side,
  As floating past their feet I go,
With nothing, save the breeze, to guide
  My tiny shallop 'mid the flow
Of rolling waters, coursing on
  To swell the billows of the sea;
But now those waters, hushed and calm,
  Seem sleeping in tranquility.

'Tis so with many a human heart,
  Which often throbs so low and still,
That from its light, exterior part,
  It seems to flow unloosed from will;
But ah! beneath that shadowy gauze,
  Wild thoughts and passions often roll,

Which know no bound'ries, save the laws
  That sway the ocean of the soul.

And now, as past the hills I drift,
  And gaze upon their frontlets high—
Which seem like genii, as they lift
  Their frowning shapes against the sky—
I picture to myself the thought
  That I am floating down life's stream ;
While all the hills seem sorrows, brought
  To mar the beauty of its dream.

And slowly now I drift, and gaze
  Upon the rocky, moonlit shore,
Where Indian maids in other days,
  Oft sat and dreamed their weird thoughts
      o'er ;
Or leaned, perchance, their bronzéd brows,
  Each on her warrior lover's breast—
Pledging, in accents low, the vows
  Which they alone could know the best.

And still I flow adown thy cheek
  Like some lost tear, O beauteous stream!
As fancy strives in vain to seek
  A tide more lovely than ye seem.
O stream! when in my boyhood's days
  I saw my portrayed face in thee,
There came no cloud to dim my gaze,
  But all was sweet simplicity.

But now the face which looketh down
  Is traced with many a line of care,
And sorrows which we cannot drown
  Have penned their names out plainly there.
Now fading fast is every dream,
  But would, O God! my life had been
For me, as calm as this loved stream—
  I'd mourn no days departed then.

THE SUNSET LAND.

Out in a beautiful land I know,
  Over a golden sea of mist,
Whose waves arise like drifts of snow,
  Dashing on shores of amethyst :—
Out in this dreamy land of mine,
  Oft I wander alone, and stand
On the brow of my Apennine,
  Gazing down on the Sunset Land.

Only in dreams I wander there—
  Only when sleep has kissed my eyes—
Then I seem but a thing of air,
  Floating beyond the chaliced skies—

Then I gather my robe of cloud
  Closer about me, as I stand
Crowned and kingly, amid the crowd,
  Gazing down on the Sunset Land.

Only there would I love to dwell—
  There, 'neath arbors of linden trees,
Pranked with tints of the asphodel,
  Round the sleeping anemones.
Now I can only grieve and pine,
  Walking with measured tread the strand—
A shore of pearl and coralline—
  Gazing down on the Sunset Land.

There the beautiful day-girl kneels,
  Washing the hills with tears of dew—
Drying them with her hair, which steals
  Softly over the ether blue:
Tresses of Sunset! oft you're bound
  By the hills with a silken band,

Gyving the azure cope around,
  In the beautiful Sunset Land.

Only there would I love to dwell—
  There in a land of ceaseless June,
Where I could tread each fairy dell,
  Plucking the fruit and wild festoon.
There, where the bright, ethereal days
  Float like banners, dreamily fanned
Down to the past, on lambent rays—
  There, in the beautiful Sunset Land.

Only there would I love to dwell,
  Where, echoing back from shore to shore,
The strains of ivory conchs would swell
  From wonderful isles of madrepore.
And cloudlets flecking the glowing skies,
  Seem but as footprints, on a strand
Bathed in billows of crimson dyes,
  In the beautiful Sunset Land.

As I stand on the Apennine,
  Gazing down on the land I know,
Oft I see, 'neath a trellised vine,
  Angels floating the dim below.
And one, whose face I oft have seen,
  Beckons me with her slender hand—
Fallen, yet beautiful Magdalen!
  Waft me down to the Sunset Land.

On me now, as in days of yore,
  Rest your eyes of violet dusk;
When soft sea breezes, on the shore,
  Breathing aromas richer than musk,
Blew your ringlets over my face,
  And the wavering verdure fanned—
Magdalen fallen—redeemed at last,
  In this beautiful Sunset Land!

So I dream of the land I know,
  Where the limning sunset rays,

Paint the mist in the dim below,
With porphyry, pearl and chrysoprase.
On the brow of the Apennine,
Oft as amid the crowd I stand,
Off from the shore of coralline,
Fades the beautiful Sunset Land.

So my joys in my dream of life,
Have faded out from a rocky shore,
And from this shadowy gyre of strife,
Have gone from me forevermore.
Soon I shall follow them o'er a sea—
O'er a ruby and agate strand—
Out to the dream revealed to me,
In the beautiful Sunset Land.

There, in that dreamy, dim unknown—
Floating beyond the purple skies—
I shall gather the wild festoon,
When another sleep has kissed my eyes.

And in the golden, shimmering sheen,
  On a sapphire and jasper strand,
I shall wander with Magdalen,
  In the beautiful Sunset Land.

VANDERLYN.

OBIIT MDCCCLII.

No tomb inscribed with storied praise,
  In thoughts which breathe a dreamy
    charm,
Nor monument, we need upraise
  To keep his memory ever warm.
His deeds are not resolved to dust—
  They know no bitter ban of doom—
They live, and still forever must,
  Though ages yield their gleam and gloom.

Now brightly, through the mist of time,
  Those works appear, of brain and heart,

And glow in cycles more sublime,
  Around the dreamy brow of Art:
Or, like those pictures grand and old,
  Whose halos light the path of fame,
They twine, in lambent rays of gold,
  An aureola round his name.

Oh! evermore that name shall be
  An astral in the cave of mind,
To light, where hid in mystery,
  The treasures of deep thought are shrined;
While, like some foamy edge of cloud,
  Whose finger points the unknown sea,
His deeds float o'er the sky of years,
  And point to immortality.

He walked the verdant meads among,
  And saw the yeoman bind the sheaves—
He wandered where the robin sung,
  While forests wept their tears of leaves;

And over all he saw a gleam,
  Like opal bathed in rubric dyes;
Then like an iris o'er his dream
  Beheld the Beautiful arise.

He drank the bitter cup that all
  Must quaff, who love this dreamy power—
He saw its dark-winged shadows fall,
  And limned them on each fleeting hour;
While through the dimly pictured whole,
  The golden germ of thought was shrined,
Which saw, deep hidden in the soul,
  The mystery of the Artist mind.

He rhymed the melody of Art,
  With mythic dreams of sea and wood;
And 'mid the ruins of his heart,
  Like Marius at Carthage, stood.
But now, upon her swelling breast
  Fair Genius bows her beauteous head,

And mourns, with hands together pressed—
  The Raphael of the age is dead.

O Vanderlyn! for thee no more
  Shall gneiss-ribbed hills, or heights unsought,
Or sea-lips, pressing on the shore,
  E'er swell thy monologue of thought.
But through that arch divinely grand,
  Where peals the clarion voice of fame,
Resounding over sea and land,
  Shall echo, evermore, thy name.

TWO MAPLES.

THE stream hath its tinkling voices,
  And the glebe its songs of seas ;
But the grandest of Nature's music
  Floats in the harps of trees.

Two vernal harps are these Maples,
  Whose melody sways and swings—
The leaves are the mystical fingers,
  And the boughs are the golden strings.

Oft when the calm of the twilight,
  In a twilight of fancy weaves,
I have wrapt myself in their music,
  As they are wrapt in leaves ;

And drinking from unseen goblets,
  Have found a calm surcease
From daily endeavor and longing,
  In the crystal draughts of peace.

Or have looked through the leafy lattice,
  And gazed on the starry scroll,
As often some wordless feeling
  Looks up to the sky of the soul!

In fervent noons, when the sunshine
  Fetters the languorous shade,
Each bandrol leaf seems a cloudlet
  Swung over a fairy glade.

While here, 'neath the spreading branches,
  I read from the bards sublime,
Whose songs are like glittering banners
  Hung on the walls of Time;

And a dreamy feeling of sadness,
  Comes over my thoughts again,
For I see in those grand old poems,
  The woven threads of pain.

Oft when the crimson of autumn,
  Is crushed on the lips of leaves,
The purples and golds of fancies
  The weary day relieves;

And the blushing cheeks of these Maples,
  Like silent clouds appear,
That are floating a long horizon,
  In the sunset of the year.

You have smiled on me your blessings,
  And taught me your lessons long,
But in return, O Maples,
  I can give you only a song!

THE PALISADES.

THE forehead of the Hudson stands,
Crowned with its shaggy locks of pines;
And sloping from the wave-washed sands,
The shore, the rocky brow confines.
The river wrapt in silence sleeps,
Swept by the eyelids of the trees;
While o'er the darkly towering steeps,
The clouds seem anchored argosies.

Long have those pillared rocks reposed,
Like some vast falchion in its sheath,
Mute, with their secrets undisclosed,
O'er that dark stream which rolls beneath.

They speak a language more sublime
  Than words can yield or fancy cast—
The unknown whisper of all time—
  The voiceless echo of the past.

Long have these silent Palisades
  Seemed phantoms stalking on the shore,
To haunt the longing which pervades
  The dreamer's soul for mystic lore;
But still they yield not up reply,
  They give not us the ecstatic bliss—
We cannot quaff the meaning high,
  Of nature's great Acropolis.

But he whose nobler thoughts confess,
  The power o'ermastering of the soul,
Who revels in the deep excess,
  Where fancy's mists of glory roll,
Sees in this colonnade of hills,
  A rhyme in nature's glad acclaim—

A meaning and a song, which thrills
  Along its dark colossal frame.

He feels the aspiring hills impart
  A passion none can e'er express,
Which steals dream-mantled from the heart,
  In awe twin-soul with happiness:
As though some mystery of the past,
  Which through the lapse of years concealed,
With all its promptings, now at last,
  By some wierd seer was unrevealed.

Ah, like these looming Palisades—
  This altar, whereon kneels the sky,
Arising 'mid the deepening shades,
  In all its vague immensity—
O ever like this, while are wrought
  The clouds of dreams which crown the whole,
May rise the Palisades of thought,
  From out the river of the soul.

Like water dripping in a cave,
  Too oft our thoughts in golden rain,
Fall in our cave-like hearts, and save
  Their pathway, naught is found again.
O speed the time in broadening streams,
  When like these hills which prop the skies,
In every soul, majestic dreams
  Of innate beauty shall arise.

Long have these silent Palisades,
  When twilights' purple dun, has hurled
Its dappled mantle down the glades,
  Seemed shadows of a giant world!
Ah, in our dreams these hills are wrought,
  In many a gyre of flight sublime,
To pure, immortal harps of thought,
  Hung on the willow trees of time.

O towering, castellated hills!
  You fill the heart with holy calm,

And breathe, like banks of daffodils,
  Ambrosial moments, dripping balm!
While round thy couch in endless charms
  The sunset curtains fall aside;
O river! in thy liquid arms,
  Is clasped thy peerless, cloud-veiled bride.

Long have these silent Palisades,
  Against the midnight's starry breast,
Wrapped in their clinging robe of shades,
  Reposed in dark, eternal rest.
And where the silver moonlight falls,
  Before those stately ramparts driven,
The grim, majestic citadels,
  Seem like the battlements of heaven.

O moonlight in the Palisades!
  The sloping shore—the fane-like steep,
And river glistening down the glades,
  Are clasped by lambent arms in sleep.

The round moon seems a fount of light,
  Whose waters rise in crystal rills,
Tinkling with silence, o'er the bright—
  The silver gardens of the hills.

Amid the emerald-mottled glades,
  Where nights' fair Peri's glance has gleamed,
Oft have these silent Palisades,
  Like some rock-worded idyl seemed.
And now beneath, meandering by,
  The dark tide seeks its goal afar,
And seems a river paved with sky,
  Whose every wave upheaves a star.

Like some old cloister, dark and grand,
  Whose beauties with its age increase,
Seem these immortal hills, which stand,
  Bathed in the litanies of peace!
Long have they, dreamy Palisades,
  By naught save variant breezes trod,

Ascended from the sloping glades,
Like incense rising up to God.

O thus, in many a silent mind,
Vague heights of deeper feeling rise,
With golden longings intertwined,
Which this life never satisfies.
But ever shall this incense loom,
Where dreams their amber waters roll;
And hearts in cycles 'mid the gloom,
Shall swing like censers in the soul.

Ah, still these ridgy Palisades,
Which Sphinx-like, rear their brows of stone
Survive the myriad decades
Of ages, down the dim past flown.
But yet the hoarded years must bow,
And pass like waves upon a sea,
Before these towering hills, which now
Are in their own eternity.

The wordless Pyramids, upon
  The desert, kneeling down to pray,
And the dead, pathetic Parthenon,
  Must with the future pass away;
But these, the eternal God-made hills,
  Whose strong foundations stand secure
Where iron decay no use fulfills,
  O, these shall evermore endure!

And I, like years, shall pass away;
  But if my dust rest 'mid the glades,
From whence shall spring from fulsome clay.
  A violet in the Palisades;
Then unto life shall I have borne,
  A type of that I worshiped well—
Then not in vain, shall I have worn
  For nature, my frail Scallop-shell.

DREAMLAND.

EIDOLON is the king,
Hear his starry gittern ring—
How its golden cadence seems
Like the sound of bells in dreams.
Hark! the voice comes wand'ring back,
Round the brazen Zodiac—
Dashing like the waves of seas,
O'er the silver Hebrides.
Borne on angel-winged delight,
Come the voices of the night—

Voices from the land of dreams.
Ultimate that Aiden gleams,
Like the worlds of thought which roll,
Through the heavens of the soul.

O'er the river of the night,
Is an amber bridge of light;
Silently it seems to stand,
Leading to a silent land—
Leading from the midnight shore,
To the dim forevermore.
As the moon-rise on the sea,
Leaves a path of mystery,
Pendant o'er the wat'ry hush,
Like the morning's primal blush,
Dashed upon the cheek of night;
So this filmy bridge of light,
O'er a waveless, unknown deep,
Stretcheth from the shores of sleep—

From dank tarns and fetid streams,
To the sylphid land of dreams.

Peering wildly into night,
Gaze I from the bridge of thought:
Beautiful transmuted light,
In mosaic fancies wrought.
Where that bridge doth rest on sleep,
Dreams their ceaseless vigils keep—
Dreams perchance of infant years.
Here the bony ghoul appears,
And with inessential hand,
Pointeth to the distant land—
To the Morning Land of Dreams.
Here the fire-eyed python gleams.
Saurians, through the murky brake,
Wander with the slimy snake.
Here the cicale wings, and sees
All the tops of upas trees
Rise like billows in the breeze.

Effete, haunted, dark and deep,
Is the silent land of sleep.

Slowly o'er the bridge I tend—
Now no livid clouds impend,
From the dim perennial morn.
On the concave's verge are born,
Jasper splendors, bearing thence,
Swathed in gold magnificence,
O'er the caverns of the night,
Gleamy, dewy drops of light.
Now an oval glow on high,
Presses 'gainst the scroll of sky,
Like the signet ring of God.
Hills of thought and dreams, untrod,
Rise before the startled view.
Golden glories glow anew.
Trembling on the bridge I stand,
Gazing o'er the Morning Land.

Music oars along the breeze,
Like the sounds of streams and trees,
Woven into melodies.
Rich aromas fill the air ;
And the dreamy everywhere,
Seems, amid the lucent shoals,
Heaven for the flowrets souls.
Here immortal beauties dwell.
Here ten thousand sunsets fell,
Which before the mythic sun,
Rose and melted into one.

In this halcyon land of bliss,
Stands a vast Metropolis.
Grandly gleam the argent fanes,
From the far, diurnal plains.
Minaret and turret high,
Tower against the topaz sky,
Over wall and bubbling dome.
Here no ghost or sullen gnome,

Ever from Erebus comes.
Here forever over us,
Float the multitudinous
Thoughts and fancies of our lives,
Here the balmy distance gyves,
With embroideries of hills,
All the gleam of molten rills.
Here the day is never done—
'Tis the Eldorado vast,
Of the future and the past—
'Tis an everlasting sun.

BURNS.

ON BEING PRESENTED WITH A LEAF FROM THE BRIGS OF AYR.

A NAME seems graven on this leaf,
  To which our memory fondly turns—
A name that brings a balm to grief—
    The name of Robert Burns.

Each leaf is vocal with his praise,
  Round Scotland's storied Brigs of Ayr—
O home of song!—"the banks and braes
    O' bonnie Doon" are there.

And there, like morning's blush which played
  On cheeks of mountains vast and tall,
His peerless Highland Mary strayed
    Around Montgomery's wall.

And there the Cotter still at eve,
  Oft bows before his humble shrine;
And still his rustic songs receive,
    The crown of Auld Lang Syne.

There Logan rolls its silver tide—
  There winds the wooded Cragie-burn—
There "Evan mingles with the Clyde,"
    And there is Dumfries' urn.

All cling around the poet's name,
  Like wreaths about the sculptured bust;
And grow immortal with his fame,
    Which moulders not to dust.

We only know his noble deeds—
The good by far out-stripped the ill—
His pride o'er-mastering, sowed the seeds
That triumphed over will.

He saw along the dreamy skies,
And over every path he trod,
An Unknown Sentiment arise,
And knew that it was God.

To him the fields new beauties wore,
New rays round Woman's pathway twined;
While in his open heart he bore
A love for all mankind.

There have been nobler themes than his,
And grander strains of that high art,
Which but the creed of nature is—
The mirror of the heart.

But ah! few ever touched the strings
He woke where depths of feeling roll—
Where round our every fancy clings
The rhythm of the soul.

How "Scots wha hae wi' Wallace bled"
Brings deep emotions to the tongue!
What memories start the tears unshed,
When Devons song is sung!

His is no idle breath of fame:
And more than Highland hearts shall raise
Round the great glory of his name,
The meed of noble praise.

O'er Scotland's sacred hills and streams,
O,er Summer dell and balmy plain,
Which float our memory haunted dreams,
His songs are heard again.

And e'en the Mountain Daisies rear
  Ambrosial praise in flowery urns,
And write on every hillside here,
    The name of Robert Burns.

THE CATSKILLS.

THE mountains overhung with gold,
  In piled luxuriance rim the view,
And seem in many an azure fold,
  Like shadows in a lake of blue.
They float through wavy gloom and glare,
  They hang like banners bright and free,
And tremble in the depths of air,
  Along the shoreless, sunset sea.

O, in the Indian-summer haze,
  They seem some long, dim reach of mist,
Along the river's liquid ways,
  Lit up with pearl and amethyst.

Or, swathed in ambient glow and green,
  When golden glories crown the skies,
They seem beneath the dædal sheen,
  The silent gates of Paradise.

O mountains, home of cliff and pine;
  Warriors of cloud-hosts drifting by!
The distance paints, in light divine,
  Your curving peaks against the sky—
The distance, ripe with glories swung
  O'er vapors in a shower of gold,
Seems like some fadeless garden, hung
  In bright carnations o'er the world.

Ah, in the conscious twilight hush,
  When shadows drink the dells of light,
The mountains, in the flickering flush,
  Seem pathless bridges o'er the night.
Aye me! O, symbols of a dream,
  Your peaks, like death, are hung between

The dawns which shall be and which seem,
  And part the dim unseen and seen.

O hills, I know your glades and dells,
  And all your crystal pools, that lie
Between the bordering asphodels,
  Each image-paven with a sky.
I know the rifts of clouds that sail
  The waveless sea of sky, and fall
Where most your rugged peaks prevail,
  Like banners round a castle wall.

O hills, the distance robes anew,
  Your forms which rise in azure dun,
And folds around your hazy blue
  The golden raiment of the sun.
O, thus each noble thought and deed,
  Rising from error's realm of night,
Shall stand, from all her bondage freed,
  Clad in immortal robes of light.

The earth is but a censer, swung
  Before the lurid throne of day;
And mist, about the mountains hung,
  Is balmy incense fumed away.
The streamlets, in the vale below,
  Diverge beside an emerald shore,
And choose new courses in their flow,
  Like lives that part and meet no more.

The boscage o'er the quiet dells,
  Inwoven with its ivy woof,
'Neath which eternal twilight dwells,
  Seems like a fairy palace roof.
A brooklet's waters rippling past,
  The vine-shaped hillside twine along,
And change to silver lakes at last,
  Like some bright fancy changed to song.

O mountains, in the summer dawns,
  When lips of light and dew have met,

I gather in your pathless lawns
  The wind-flower and the violet.
And, dreaming dreams within a dream,
  I know the daisies growing high,
To you of azure robed in gleam,
  Are what the stars are to the sky.

O hills, I know the chasm wide,
  And copse wherein comes sparkling up
The waters of a tiny tide—
  A fay within a lily's cup.
I know your varied forms which rise,
  In wavy slopes, whose trackless way
Mounts upward to the summer skies,
  And seems like dreamland seen by day.

And I, when years have passed, shall come
  Like some worn pilgrim to a shrine,
And view once more the mountain home
  Of beetling peak and towering pine;

And see the hills, impearled with dew,
  Which all the pansy nooks infold,
Again arise along the view—
  A moveless pageant robed in gold.

Then shall the streamlet in the dell,
  In whose clear lymph the shade is cast
Of many a floweret's crimson bell,
  Be but a memory of the past.
Then shall I, in the balmy glade
  Which dwells o'erarched with boughs and
      sky,
Tread where in vanished hours I strayed,
  And wake once more the days gone by.

But I shall go to rest—and when
  This fleeting dream of life is o'er,
Still to the changing race of men
  These hills shall stand forevermore.

Still shall the mountains which arise,
  Though we may be no more, alas!
Loom upward to the trackless skies,
  And mock the ages as they pass.

AMONG THE FLOWERS.

In royal dawns, alone I tread
  By pebbled brook, and shining strand,
  By vernal meadow, lone woodland,
Where queenly flowerets, from a bed
  Of dewy glory, rise to greet
  The morn with golden-sandaled feet;
And, with the day-sea overhead,
  I watch the ships of shimmer meet.

Ah, rich with cinnamon and palm,
  My dreams go out to eastern rooms—
  To orange groves, whose ceaseless blooms,
Are swaying in eternal balm ;

But yet the daisies that I see,
Bring back my truant dreams to me:
An island in a lake of calm,
Is every petaled brilliancy.

Each pansy is a pure delight,
Torn from some heart, and given form;
And beckons on the dewy morn,
Swayed in the shadow-breath of night.
And here, beneath the coppice shade,
A hushed, acacia lake is laid,
Whose waves of petals, capped with light,
Throb up the shore-like everglade.

With saddened thoughts, I wander by
A sloping glen, whose ways I know
Are strown with wreaths of jasper glow—
An aisled cathedral, broad and high,
Where, like an organ's trembling word,
The melodies of every bird,

In golden notes float up the sky—
  Sweet rapture, not from me deferred.

Ah me, when I shall be no more,
  I crave that here my couch be made,
  Beneath the turf, where sheen and shade
Shall surge the bright, dew-paven shore—
  Where dawn, the gauzy breath of day,
  Shall light this overbraided way,
And sail its sea of flowerets o'er,
  As zephyrs sail the sea of May.

Here shall each robin seem a rose,
  Which gathers life from fields of air;
  With gloom for streamlets ever fair,
And dreamy dells that woo repose,
  Beside the hills—a kingly throng;
  While warbled strains shall float along,
Where light with beauty overflows,
  And be but fragrance changed to song.

Here shall the pale narcissus, hung
  Where lilac-blooms perfume its bowers,
  Be but the rayless dawn of flowers,
In varied shades of opal, swung
  Above a tiny, bluebell hill;
  Whose valley lieth deep and still,
The emerald skies of leaves among,
  Which verge the crystal of the rill.

I crave that here my couch be made,
  For here is nature's reign supreme ;
  And here the morning-tinted stream,
Which eddies through the osier glade,
  Is like a memory that I know—
  A sainted memory, pure as snow
Upon the breasts of wild-flowers laid,
  Which blossomed where the violets blow.

The fruit is springing from the seeds—
  I know what goal my dreams have won—

And pride, which bows itself to none,
Grew o'er my hidden griefs, like weeds.
Errors are titled truths—the hours
Quaffed from the chalice, Time, are ours
Alone, with that dim path, which leads
To quiet rest beneath the flowers.

ISAURE.

At the tryst near the broken stile,
  Holding her hand in mine, I said,
  Not in the dells of shade I tread,
Not in the full-blown daisy's smile,
    Not in the twilight calm and gray,
I see the beauty that I adore;
  But in the summer of your eyes,
  Where the billows of soul arise,
Gleaming upon their tender shore,
    I clasp the dreams of endless May.

Beauty dwelleth in soul alone—
  As fruit and frondage, spice and palm,
  Dwell but in fervent isles of balm—
Yours to me is the central throne:
    Lesser glories bow down to thee;

Here the lake, like a silver vail,
  Ripples between the fallow meads,
  Islanded oft with drooping reeds—
But this is of the ships that sail,
    Brightly, out to a beautiful sea.

Your soul is the beautiful sea,
  With coral isles of golden dreams,
  And many a mystic thought which seems
Like some shadowy cave to me,
    Leading down from a pearly vale.
Here the moon, in a downy cloud,
  Seems like a bee in an asphodel,
  Whose foamy petals sink and swell
Before each languid zephyr bowed,
    Trembling beneath its ornate mail.

And here the mellow lips of light
  Kiss the sweet foreheads of the leaves,
  While some melodious night-bird weaves

Its song along its trackless flight,
 Like life—a swallow-flight of time:
But dreams were naught were thou not here:
 They are the rivers of the sea—
 The sapphire paths that lead to thee,
Through lawny lands I hold most dear,
 By thy soul-beauty made sublime.

Isaure, as some cape of cloud
 Grows brighter with the birth of day,
 So all my fancies grow to May,
Before thy purer presence bowed,
 Which seems a ceaseless dawn to me;
And our lone hearts still float in dreams,
 Like leaves in odors rustling fair,
 Which drift along the rosy air,
Like sprays of woodbine, down the streams
 That widen to the summer sea.

OCTOBER RAIN.

OCTOBER skies are pale and sere;
The ashen clouds are grim and chill—
Like ghostly mourners at a bier,
They kneel upon the distant hill.
Like leaves their freight goes hastening by;
The cold wind shouts in dizzy pain:
We know that as the moments fly,
The month is dying in the rain.

But through a tattered woof of cloud,
The sunlight slants a living glow,
Which, sparkling round the misty shroud,
Lights up the grainless fields below.

The dead leaves launched in gusts go by;
  But ah! in ruby drops divine,
The upturned goblet of the sky,
  Pours forth the rain like golden wine.

The dahlia, last of all her race,
  Puts out her lips to quaff the bliss,
As some clear lake with tender grace
  Receives the moonlight's silver kiss.
The vernal crucible of hills,
  Wherein the gold of May was laid,
Is rimmed with wild flowers round the rills,
  In pearly drops of rain arrayed.

The mountains in the dewy breath,
  Against a breast of dark cloud lie,
Which bends above them, as in death,
  The weeping mistress of the sky!
While here the sunlight's crimson bars,
  Begem the fields in amber crowds;

The starlight is the soul of stars;
  And O, the rain is soul of clouds.

The bright red berries gleaming, cling
  Above green dells of fairy birth,
And seem like twinkling stars that swing
  Above the emerald hills of earth.
I see them through the mist and rain—
  The mountains and the cloudy sky;
But dream the dead past o'er again—
  We are alone, my soul and I.

It whispers me in vague surmise,
  Some subtle meaning to impart,
That from the mind's o'er-arching skies,
  The cold rain falleth on the heart.
Our memories like the wind sweep by;
  But ah! we weep them not in vain—
Nor those who in their last sleep lie;
  For tears are but October Rain.

As through some window stained with gold,
  Which lights the weary, kneeling crowd,
In some cathedral, grand and old,
  I see the sunlight through the cloud.
And now to tell that Spring was here,
  Alone the luscious fruits remain,
Which droop from branches crisp and sere,
  Adorned with drops of golden rain.

My life has been a rainy day,
  In which some sapphire sunlight shone;
But that too soon has passed away,
  And left me to the storm alone.
It matters not—each cloud foretells
  Some brighter hours will come again,
And memory seems a harp, which swells
  With strains of sad, October Rain.

MEADOW MIST.

THROUGH fields of sparry grass and grain,
  When dawns their misty garments bring,
I walk and pluck the flowers again—
  The joyous syllables of Spring.
Now are the regal daisy bowers,
  By skies of folded vapor kissed;
Creation weeps in golden showers,
  But smileth through her tears in mist.

The forest, in the distance, seems
  A land where balmy winds abound,
Which float like music heard in dreams,
  That dies upon the breast of sound;

The jasper rivers of the sun,
The lotus sprays of mist drift o'er,
And, mottled with vermilion dun,
Are stranded on this meadow shore.

As some clear moon hangs o'er a lake,
Glassed in its waters deep and cool,
A silver lily near the brake,
Is pictured in an elfin pool—
So in a leaf-waved lake of dew,
By shores of endless morning kissed,
The vapor's image wavers through,
And seems like moonlight fumed in mist.

Upon a laurel shore remains
The daisy, like a sounding shell;
While here, the blue-eyed gentian reigns,
Queen floweret of a palace dell.
Yet over all the meadows fair,
The wavy sheens of vapor lie;

And seem like locks of amber hair,
  Swept down the forehead of the sky.

And so I pass, when breaks the day,
  Along the meads with glory rife,
And dream the lucent morn away,
  As I have dreamed the morn of life.
Not all in gold and amethyst,
  Are even summer days enshrined:
My heart hath had its share of mist—
  The sadness of a darkened mind.

All things find type in life or death:
  The landscape of the past I see;
While in the thought, this skyey breath,
  Becomes the mist of memory.
And dreaming, down by mere and shoal,
  I know—all truth some sadness yields—
As sorrow falls upon the soul,
  So vapor falleth on the fields.

MY PALACE.

In thoughts' dominions, halo-crowned,
I saw a Palace broad and high:
No streams of liquid moonlight round—
No pansies formed of azure sky.
But all of crystal glare and shade,
And snowy dells of sheen were there,
Impearling with its glowing glade,
My royal Palace in the air!

The shadowy-penciled vales and hills,
Of space and depth and dazzling height,
Lie lucent in the blazoned rills,
Which empty in a bay of light.

I see above a mount, whose dun
  Seems shade and glory mingled there;
The amber-crowned king-seraph, sun,
  With pinion winged in golden air!

And ah, this mountain evermore,
  White-robed with snow, in its high place,
Hath seemed upon the mighty shore,
  A billow from the sea of space.
Above the wave-mount's icy leas—
  Before the endless sunset skies,
With jacinth architrave and frieze
  I see my royal Palace rise.

While up the battlemented wall,
  The silken banners flaunt and flare,
O'er sapphire tower and turret tall—
  Bright vapors on the fane of air.
Turkois, agate and chrysoprase,
  Are irised round the open door;

Through which with songs of other days,
  The winged Hours pass forevermore.

The rooms within are fair to see,
  By tender gales of odor fanned,
Greek-lined with niche and filigree,
  And hung with woofs of Samarcand.
The pink-hued radiance crushed to shape,
  We call the rose, is vased around;
While from some far off mountain cape,
  The zephyrs wake the sylph of sound.

And she in whose dear eyes and mien
  I see the halo from her heart,
Of all my Palace is the queen,
  And of its beauty forms a part.
She, languorous with musk and bloom,
  Reclines where tinkling fountains pour,
Or wanders through the damasked room,
  Along the velvet-tufted floor,

Her fancies are a flower, whose green,
  Dark stem of thought, the bulb thought meets;
And she before the conscious sheen,
  Is queen-bee in a dell of sweets.
She rests on cushions wrought with sprays,
  And revels in the sunset beams:
The golden circle of her days,
  Is made ideal in her dreams.

The hours are mists which float away:
  She views where floods of ruby run,
The cloud-tinged opal of the day,
  Red-hearted with the lambent sun.
But when she sleeps, alas, I see
  The vague ghosts clothed in shade go by;
And beckoning shadowy hands to me,
  They pass the sleeper with a sigh.

O Palace on the hills of air!
  I see each tower and turret shine

And glitter, with its vestal glare
  Of chrysolite and almandine.
But ah, beneath the gleaming fane,
  Unseen, and lost to human eyes,
Dead forms in vaulted tombs remain,
  From which the flitting ghosts arise.

The soul's the Palace of the dream,
  In jasper walls of fancy wrought,
Before the sad past's sunset gleam,
  Upon the lumined hills of thought.
And oft the shadowy memories start,
  And tremble in the mystic air,
Arising from the vaulted heart—
  The ghosts of dead hopes buried there.

AT THE WATERFALL.

The shore-lips of this odorous vale—
By liquid cadence fringed with calm,
Which woos through fields the scented gale—
Are parted in the dells of balm,
And tremble with a worldless psalm,
Whose strains above the hush prevail.

The murmur of the Waterfall—
The hum of lily-shrouded bee,
And throstle's honey-throated call,
Change all the air to melody;
While wave-like in the mystic sea,
Arise the mountains vague and tall.

And now beside the endless pour—
  Where nature's life-blood, from her heart
Of throbbing emerald, runneth o'er—
  I watch the ripples, as they start
  Toward the brink, and there depart;
O life! thy type forevermore.

I see the crystal falls array
  The leaves like seraphim, with wings
Of dewy lace, from whorls of spray;
  And know the cataract now swings,
  A curtain, held with sunbeam rings,
Across the temple of the day.

And where upon the moss-crowned height,
  The watery vesture of the dell,
Sweeps down and mingles with the light,
  The sapphires of an iris dwell,
  And seem an arch of asphodel,
Where some king glow-worm passeth, bright.

So o'er each heart doth rise elate,
  The rainbow of some fond desire;
And we, frail buffeters of fate,
  Toward the dream alone aspire,
  But find that as we struggle higher,
'Tis nobler to be good than great.

But here beneath the dash and roar,
  Where eddies circle in a bay,
White-breasted lilies near the shore,
  Waste their pure snow upon the spray;
  The passion of whose lips, arrays
Each flower with gems of madrepore.

And here the amorous arms of sheen,
  Clasp their sweet presence round a cress,
Which sinks into them, rich with green,
  And faints of its dear happiness:
  While like some moonlight's silver tress,
The sunlit Waterfall is seen.

In swirls the downy mists exhale,
  Like fragrance from a dying rose,
And o'er the pearly falls prevail,
  To meet the balmy breath that blows
  The wild flowers from their soft repose,
To tremble in the tender gale.

O haste the years which still remain,
  When like these vapors which arise,
And float in orient o'er the plain
  Beneath the azure of the skies,
  This life in robes of royal dyes,
Shall to some greater good attain.

Lo, nature is for one and all;
  Her language whispers in a leaf—
The stars—the sun—a mountain tall—
  The flowers—or in a ripened sheaf;
  And a whole tome of true belief,
Dwells even in a Waterfall.

MY HARP.

A silence like a silver chain,
  Still o'er my cherished harp is cast.
I seek the urn of time again
  Which holds the ashes of the past.
One chord is severed on my lyre,
  With fairy utterance once rife—
One chord which woke a pure desire,
  Is broken on the lyre of life.

A gentle hand which long ago
  Was folded on a pulseless breast,
Freed the bird music, wild and slow,
  That fluttered o'er this harp for rest.

But through the sad past, dim and far,
  A face shines out from wreath and curl,
And bends above me like a star—
  Gleam-winged Astarte clad in pearl.

The mystic odor of her eyes
  Oft fanned my soul with honey balm,
As 'neath the great harp of the skies,
  We drifted o'er a lake of calm.
We sailed across the night, and she
  Woke from her lyre its strains divine ;
And bending with her lips o'er me
  Their purple cadence fell on mine.

She called all flowers the petaled notes
  Of lost strains in a perfume choir,
Whose sound in rarest savor floats ;
  And thought the fields, the emerald lyre.
Each tendril with its calyx blows,
  To her, sweet rapture would impart:

Perchance the soul of some dead rose,
  Held fragrant converse with her heart.

The sunset is a jacinth lyre
  With chords of ruby rays of light,
Whose melody, in strains of fire,
  Dies on the twilight breast of night :
And she whose being caused the years
  In 'wildering sweetness to depart,
Now like a silent harp appears,
  But is the sunset of my heart.

TO THE SOUTH WIND.

FROM bowery islands come, O South!
  Where dark myrrh-thickets, crowned with
    dew,
  In musky hollows bow to you,
  And touch some flower of misty blue,
To hear from out its petal mouth:
  O sweetest breeze that ever blew!

Delicious balm! with southern night
  Tint the blown grape and paint the bloom;
  And for the clover-buds make room,
  Which sway in ceaseless grief and gloom,
And weep dew-tears of lost delight,
  Above some pansy's simple tomb.

The soft, white arms of each pale rose,
Woo thee I know to peaceful rest ;
Near sedgy banks, the hawthorn's breast,
Tempts thy parched lips to nectar blessed,
Like lilies which, white-winged, arose
And passed into the silent west.

The moss-rose, 'neath her hood of green,
Blushing, doth often meet thee here,
Beside the limit of the mere,
Where jets the flag, whose blades appear,
Swayed o'er the lymph with shade between,
Like waving plumes above a bier.

A cloudy shallop floateth by—
Borne o'er the summer sea of space,
To drift thee, with its sails of lace,
To this, O gale! thy resting place ;
But in the palace of the sky,
The bright cloud seems a lighted vase.

Sweet dove! beneath thy perfume wings,
  Dost bring no message from thy clime?
  No dear words of thy tender prime?
  Does she, who in that younger time,
I loved, alas! now dwell where clings
  Her cloud-land to the hills sublime?

Perchance she lives! If so, increase
  Her wavering grace—her life employ—
  Let no marred hope her hope destroy,
  Nor the sad past her dreams annoy;
Her golden bowl be rimmed with peace,
  And beaded with white bells of joy.

The griffins at the marble stair,
  Had scarce a stonier heart than she—
  Her love the sweeter mystery:
  Oft wandering by the placid sea,
From odor clouds in carmine air,
  She showered her rose-bud lips on me.

DUE

If this book is not returned on or before the above date a fine of five (5) cents per day will be incurred by the borrower.

When you have finished reading this book do not wait until the time limit has expired, but return it to the library as soon as possible. Someone is waiting to read it.

GENERAL LIBRARY
University of Michigan
Form 96 (7-12-23) 75,000

Dear rain! unknown to darkened days
  Which rippled in the past, and swam
  Like watery circles into calm;
  This zephyr, with its robe of balm,
Recalls thee, as adown these ways,
  I dream of sandal and of palm.

In copses here uncoil the ferns,
  To couch, O South! thy limbs in ease,
  Where, 'mid the hum of mites and bees,
  Thy life shall change to one with these:
Ah! e'en the bolder yarrow learns,
  Where fraught with honey comes the breeze.

Sweet breath! half memory, half balm,
  Thou wanderest from a dell yet dear,
  Where souls of withered roses near,
  Hung sadly o'er the vernal bier,
Till some bird woke the fragrant calm,
  And fanned the perfume to me here.

WAITING.

Sentinel trees whose spears are stars,
Guard the lawn and its pebbled way;
And through the boughs, like emerald bars,
The moon pours down its silver day.
The grange seems cut against the sky,
Lights in the windows glow and gleam;
I fear you care but little, that I
Am waiting for you, Marian Dreem

Sadly I watch the fragrant flame
Of flowers, which seem like burning ships,
And, breathing now thy honeydew name,
Silk-belted bees hum round my lips.

The orange blooms seem dead and cold,
  Withered and dead with dripping dew:
Is love forgot, or love grown old?
  Marian sweet, I shall question you.

I meet you first in a vale of calms,
  Of listless deeps and fluted gloom,
A valley brimmed with a thousand balms,
  Where luscious dusk was rich perfume.
And where the flushed day reared its throne
  On flaccid billows of crimson shine,
The sky by an Odin-breath was blown
  To a bubble of purple wine.

There the sweet, south zephyr faints in heat,
  By the dear, parched mouth of Summer
    kissed;
And where the clouds of porphyry meet,
  They seem a city shaped in mist—
A city of some embodied bliss
  Built in the future, seen through thought:

If other dreams are fair as this,
 Marian sweet, must ours be naught?

Well, you can make me pale with a look,
 Or say in kisses you're still my own;
Standing here by the naze-crowned brook,
 I'm yet at our wonted tryst alone.
Waiting and watching, I fear the worst—
 Waiting and watching, echoes the stream,
But I, though you make my life accursed,
 Sadly shall love you, Marian Dreem.

Then I shall have my gifts again,
 Soul print letters, necklace and ring;
But you never shall know the pain
 That even their poor presence will bring.
But all my doubts are frail as air,
 I hear a step in the dell beneath;
The orange blossoms seem fresh and fair—
 I see them twined in a bridal wreath.

AGLAIA.

UNLOOSE your hair from its russet braids ;
Let it descend like silken dew,
'Neath the skies of your eyes of blue,
And mingle down, with gathering shades,
Over your shoulders of pearly white.
I hear the fount's incanting fall
In billow-cadence from the hall,
And a distant gittern's symphonies.
All things murmur a hushed delight,
Sweet mystery of mysteries!

Starlight floats round thee like a vail—
Each tress seems sunshine in repose—
Here the ruby flame of a rose

Kisses thy breast to an amorous gale,
And burns with a passionate soul!
  I gaze from oriels tinted red—
  This silver cresset, naptha-fed,
    Floods the room with malachite seas.
Filled to the brim is the golden bowl,
    Fair mystery of mysteries!

Come out into the night, sweet dream!
  To vernal silence by the lake,
  Where moonlight falleth flake by flake,
And white flowers forever seem,
On the lips of the liquid gloom,
  A lily-Venice rich and rare.
  Come down the lane where, cowled in air,
    All the whispering linden trees
Count their chaplets in beads of bloom,
    Loved mystery of mysteries!

Come, flashing with diamonds and lace,
  To bosky dells where, overhead,

A single circle of silver thread,
Arches above the young moon's face,
And seems a dome—the far-off sign
Of the glimmering city of stars.
Come where no baser fancy mars
The higher life of reveries.
Come, my beautiful! mine, still mine,
Fair mystery of mysteries!

Here, in this elfin nook, we rest—
You breathe an influence vague and strange,
To balmful Edens of sense; and change
Like clouds along the purple west.
Here a daisy upon the shore,
Like a radiant soul doth seem,
Waiting to cross the Stygian stream.
With fragrant spirits such as these,
You hold communion evermore,
Sweet mystery of mysteries!

Thou wast a bird whose regal notes,
  Though changed to voice, are still the same.
  Thy warm, rich beauty soothes, aflame—
Ecstatic sweetness ever floats,
Where'er its eastern spell is cast.
  If hopes were strong as fairy ships,
  I'd waste my being on thy lips,
    Here, sailing life's midsummer seas
And mingle with thee and the past,
    Dear mystery of mysteries!

ON THE LAKE.

THE glassy stillness of the mere,
  In samite tapestries of shade,
Dents the hushed coves: while pale and clear,
  A bridge of moonlight spans the glade.
A starry cestus zones o'erhead;
  Blue Lyra, harp of Israfel,
  Lights the pure peace: in balm doth dwell
Antares, flashing snow and red.

I launch my boat upon the lake,
  And drift along the liquid dark,
To watch in brier or woven brake,
  The fire-fly sail his vermeil bark.

Some night-bird drips a note through night,
To surge the dusky silence o'er;
Where daisies yield upon the shore,
Their melody of gold and white.

An angel laves a pool of thought,
And makes a cherished memory whole;
A brain-mist falls, with silver fraught,
And eyes peer out which type a soul.
While, bound with pearls in wavy gloom,
The hair floats down: a spangled dream;
And cheeks joy-fervent, ever seem
Flushed like some sweet pomegranate bloom.

No sound is heard: the jasper dew,
Torn from the tissue of a cloud,
Floods a meek pansy's eyes of blue,
Which o'er a frail wind-flower is bowed.
The violet odor seems to say,
In spicy tones to sadness moved:

Ah me! to love and not be loved,
Sets starlight in the breast for day.

In respite from a painless death,
This spray of mint no more shall stir,
Nor wrap the incense of its breath,
Around the spiky lavender.
A tuberose seems a mimic May,
And with caught sunlight forms a part.
Saying: There dwells in every heart,
A hidden idol draped away—

The sun is idol of the flowers.
I drift along the tepid June,
And read afar from placid bowers,
The mystic missal of the moon.
I float the lake and watch the dells,
Obedient to the variant tide,
Where dim and ghostly shadows glide
Along the brink, like sentinels.

Earth is the altar of the night,
  Whose jeweled ephod is the sky,
And flowers the offering to light,
  For whose dear sake they live to die.
All valley-bowered from the breeze,
  The lake is strange to wave or whorl,
  And seemeth like a liquid pearl,
Amid the tresses of the trees.

Ah, many a life is like this mere,
  Rich with an innate mystery,
And dark and rare, but calm and clear,
  And purer than the common sea.
Such lives that, striving after truth,
  Before dear nature's sceptered throne
  Of beauty bow, O such alone,
Have glimpses of immortal youth!

Where myrtle-blossoms fleck the green
  Of thymy banks, I see the light

Edge the still lake with lily sheen,
  Like beaded clouds which fringe the night.
And dew-drops sparkle in each glome,
  By purple bays in maple glens,
  While o'er the depths and in the fens,
The glow-worms dash their diamond foam.

Here odors, tinged with dusk, arise
  From nard and cassia, frail and thin,
And mingle 'neath the leafy skies,
  Like sounds of lute and mandolin.
If always by such balmy shore,
  And with no ruder breezes pressed,
  Life's waters might serenely rest,
How sweet to live for evermore!

SEPTEMBER TO APRIL.

You are a white vein in a shell—
  A dew-drop hid in the breast of a rose—
  A leaf that sinks in a brook as it flows—
A fay in a lily's silver bell,
  Or a dell by a river, in green repose.

I am robed in russet and gold;
  I dwell in crofts, and a fall which pours
  White lilies of spray upon its shores.
I am dying 'mid wealth untold;
  The breeze is the splash of the golden oars!

Green fields babble in flowers to you;
  You are morning-star of the years—
  The Nereid which spring-barked appears.

Roses are sweetest in the dew,
  And you in silvery, silken tears.

The snow is a vail 'twixt thee and me ;
  It keepeth thy lips from mine alway.
  You and I are clouds of a day,
Which, drifting over the crimson sea,
  In pearls of white perfume waste away.

The diamond-smile of odorous stars,
  Hangeth thy skies with joy for thee.
  You, in the sunset of time, shall be
One of the radiant jasper bars,
  And a bead on a mystic rosary.

Oh, my beautiful! we but swing,
  Like fragrant censers, up and down.
  You paint the green and I the brown.
You are the gem in the zone of Spring,
  And I the Autumn's golden crown.

JUNE MEMORIES.

ONLY some memories of June :
  What time the fish leap in the firth,
  The fanged-bug haunts the leafy girth,
And locusts pour their drowsy tune—
When plovers pipe along the brink
  By silver shores in pearly shine,
Where gorgeous insects come to drink
  From cups of tulips, brimmed with wine.

Then rich moss-roses star the plats,
  And in dim dawns, on dewy boughs,
  The joyous brown-thrush trills his vows
In alder clumps and willow flats.

Then near the growths of mistletoe,
  Where cuckoos chant their love-sweet cry,
Dear bands of violets I know,
  In odor dreams, go up the sky.

Some say, the morn of memory
  Is ever dropping tender dew;
  I know not if the thought be true,
But yet, some sadness falls on me.
For few can look on vanished days,
  However bright their suns have set,
And say: I see but cause to praise,
  And find no reasons for regret.

Like shade on pinks at heated noon,
  Where cooling breezes seldom blew,
  The past casts down its healing dew,
And makes my dream a peaceful June.
As swings a sparrow on a spray,
  The memory sways, nor errant, flies,

While on the verge, and far away,
 The almonds of Avilion rise.

I see the twilight glooming down ;
 And Hesper, in the azure sky,
 Seems like a blue-bell's amber eye,
Or like a blue-bell's golden crown.
Then, soon from depths of purple-black,
 Orion glimmers forth with Mars,
And all the Pleiads, flashing back,
 Are gold grapes, clustered 'mid the stars.

A trailer's leaflet holds with care
 A crimson berry on its gloom,
 And seems a beryl urn, whose plume
Of spiced flame wavers in the air.
Then comes a day with cloud-vailed face,
 Whose mists robe white the mountains high,
But leave their peaks to swing in space—
 The hanging gardens of the sky.

I see June on the moor and wold :
  The martins eddy round the limes ;
  And like a dream of fairer climes,
Arises each marsh-marigold.
The month doth whisper from the grass—
  It floats the day and its decline.
My heart seems but a slanted glass,
  Filled to the brim with June, like wine.

Ah sweet, when first the rose in tears
  Of dew, burst open to the sun!
  But soon its petals one by one,
Had fallen in the stream of years ;
And all its song-bird's tender tune
  Had fled—its flowerets ceased to grow ;
For life, alas! has but one June—
  October beckons, and I go.

RETURNED FROM WAR.

Shrouded by his country's flag,
And in martial garments dressed,
Came the soldier to his home,
With his sword upon his breast.

Stepping to the muffled drum,
Pass the guard on either side :
All the people as they come,
Whisper how the warrior died.

Of his deeds, what words can tell ?
But in battle, 'mid the van,
Cheering on the fight, he fell
For the common cause of man.

He shall lead the charge no more—
  Scale the rampart to the gun ;
For they bear him gently home,
  To his wife and little one.

She, who through her bridal vail,
  Looked and called him dearest, best!
Bends above him in her tears,
  With her head upon his breast.

She has sorrow for her part :
  Grief alone to her is sent,
Blighting all her summer heart,
  And the roses of content.

What if victory crowned the day ?
  She will heed you not nor stir :
He has fallen in the fray :
  He was all the world to her.

LADY LISLE.

THE Lady Lisle is fair and good ;
  Her grace, like spikenard spilt ; her ways,
Surmounting all the pride of blood :
  She holds her peace unless to praise ;
All love her perfect womanhood.

The landscape-painter from afar,
  Unconscious, in his toil immersed,
Is dearer than all others are ;
  She sees and loves him from the first ;
His face shines on her like a star.

She leaves her house at golden dawn ;
  Her gardener's makes her dwelling place :
She whispers that her wealth is gone ;
  She lays aside her pearls and lace,
And puts a simple kirtle on.

'Twas June when kindly nature smiled—
A queen of roses was the day:
The painter half the morn beguiled,
To meet her in the village way,
But knew her as the gardener's child.

He quaffed delight with half a fear;
He scorned the dross of ignorant wealth;
So, in the rose-month of the year,
He wooed her for her dower of health,
And for her goodness, held her dear.

He gave a sketch of peace, which shed
A brighter halo on his name;
Peace rested in the blue o'erhead—
Peace on the lake and hill the same;
And peace within his breast, he said.

She praised his work—true work of Art;
And praise from such sweet lips was bliss.

I love, he said ; and for her part,
  She gave him with a loving kiss,
Her trust, the warder of her heart.

When dusk had twined, with ruby shine,
  The star-flowers in the hair of night,
He spoke of tilt and royal line,
  And mentioned with subdued delight,
His vine-clad cottage on the Rhine.

The bridal dawn in many a smile
  Was wreathed, that blushed forth into day.
She said, while in the chapel aisle,
  The gardener's child has passed away—
She was, and is, the Lady Lisle.

He saw her jewels' shade and shine ;
  And proudly stood he up and said,
Though Lady Lisle, you still are mine,
  And shall be, after we are wed,
The Countess Aura on the Rhine.

LEGEND OF THE KAATERSKILL.

LIKE a stone with an inscription,
  'Gainst the sepulchre of night,
With its halo of tradition,
  Garden Rock is garnished bright.
Here the Manitou or Spirit
  Reared the palace of the dawn,
When the stars, the sleeping beauties,
  Trembled ere the dark was gone.
Here he gave the valleys plenty,
  To the seaboard far away;
Here he breathed his wrath in tempests,
  Here he smiled his love in day.

At the base, dank, turbid waters
  Filled the hollow in a lake;

And beside each tiger-lily
  Lay a lizard or a snake.
Far around the sloping margin,
  Flowers in wild luxuriance grew;
Hyacinths of snow and azure,
  Roses swathed in crimson dew.
Then at times some flashing robin
  Through the woodland sailed along,
Seeming like a bark with banners
  Floating down a tide of song.

So the Indians loved the precinct,
  With a sacred awe and fear;
And the bravest of the hunters,
  Never dared to enter here.
'Till one autumn dusk, when Nature
  Mild in all her aspect lay,
One who clambered up the mountain,
  Passed within the haunted way.
Here a mystic sense stole o'er him,
  He had never known before,

As he watched the broad pond-lilies,
  Like white sails afar from shore.

Here the lark to sleep was nestled.
  First to wake at ruddy gleam ;
And the presence of the poppies
  Wrought each sorrow in a dream.
To the Indian, all the twilight
  Bridged a feeling vague and deep ;
While his soul in thoughts of beauty,
  Charmed with silence, seemed to sleep.
But he saw, o'er moss and lichen,
  Every tulip's fiery crest,
And they seemed like travelers murmuring :
  Alabama. Here we rest.

Lost and prostrate now, the hunter
  Changing to a spring did seem ;
Then adown the mountain's bosom,
  Like a ringlet fell a stream!
Eadem semper; for the noblest

Who to greatest heights attain,
Find the pleasure-pain of knowledge—
But are dashed to earth again.
They have found the fount a Mara,
Still receding in the ken;
But their thoughts, in living waters,
Wander through the hearts of men.

So the streamlet down the valley,
Laughed in ripples in the sun,
Purling o'er the distant reaches,
When the day had just begun.
While, in spiral whirls, the bittern
Sailed its lonely way along,
Drinking in the scents of roses,
Where they bourgeon in a throng.
And the Indian's deathless spirit,
Wrapped in golden languors still,
Whispers bliss in every murmur
Of the crystal Kaaterskill.

THE RIVER-SIDE.

I TAKE the path where none intrude—
  A sparry line by thorp and sted—
And in a wave-lipped solitude,
  Tinct with flushed spring-time overhead,
I watch the hills whose feet are shores:
  In crystal calms their shadow lies,
Which seem like marble palace floors,
  Roofed with the arras of the skies.

The silken buds are on each tree:
  Dear birds their pent-up rapture sing:
While flowery banners wave to me,
  And petal bells sweet welcome ring.

The Spring breaks through the fading rime ;
  Once more she robes these banks for you,
With glories of a fairer clime,
  Oh, River, sister of the dew !

Oh, River, sister of the sea,
  Flow down, and all thy being pour
Into thy brother's arms, to be
  A type of time for evermore.
For each year leads to greater ends :
  The future dawns with brighter smiles,
And fate, a veering shallop, tends
  To summer seas and jasper isles.

To dare is half what 'tis to do—
  So, ever daring for the right,
Keeping some noble aim in view,
  Let each strive onward with his might.
Then social ills will soon assuage—
  Then life will not be dead at heart,

But time soon bring th' Elysian age
  When Use shall take the hand of Art.

Oh, River! mother of the rain,
  Along your brink spiced flowers abound,
And here a lily blooms again—
  An ivory lyre, with fragrant sound.
Ah! even a bud with perfume breath,
  Is with a holy lesson rife ;
For life is but the germ of death,
  And death, the bud of higher life.

And so I dream with calm delight,
  And watch the River sparkle by,
Till, like a ripened autumn, night
  Has strown, with golden leaves, the sky.
Now, though I go, I know whene'er
  I see bright waters glide and gleam,
I'll fancy once again I hear
  Thy silver dash of waves, oh stream!

DORA.

Now for the first in six long years, I stood
Beside my cousin, Dora, at the Hall—
A gray old grange which mocked the errant
years;
Its features English, as my uncle's were—
The dear God give him peace, for he is dead.
Dora the woman, statelier than the girl,
Shook hands, and placed her husband's fast
in mine,
Saying to him:
"Oh, Vivian! though he once
Made stalking shadows of three weary
years,
Forgive, forgive my cousin for my sake."

Strange words: and when I asked the sense,
They both threw out a hundred butterflies
Of questions of the time since last we met,
Which flew for answer round and round my
ears;
And Dora set her child upon my knee,
Which had its mother's eyes and golden hair.

Soon after, Vivian thus: "At times, I write
To quell the waking dream that life oft' seems;"
So, to explain the vague words of his wife,
He read a poem, three years old that day—
Written on visiting the quaint, old Hall,
After my uncle's death, with Dora gone:—

At the angle of the path,
Plays the fountain in the air:
Swans are in a crystal bath;
Roses in the sweet parterre.

In the glamour and the shine,
  Drowse the peacocks on the wall,
Where the sprays of eglantine,
  O'er the marble Daphne fall.

Memory clingeth to the scene,
  And the lily-clouded cope;
On the past she seems to lean—
  That her anchor, she a Hope.

For across a silent sea,
  Flashes gleam along the shore—
Dreams of one who is to me,
  Queen of days that are no more.

Here close-linked at eve, we saw
  Branchy shadows braid the walk;
And with civic strife and law
  Mingled in discursive talk.

She had dreamy, harebell eyes,
  Sunning o'er a faultless face—

Soul-deeps for her low replies,
  And a form of perfect grace.

When the night hung balanced near,
  Oft we took this dusky lawn;
And the starry circle here,
  Seemed the wedding-ring of dawn.

When at eve we lingered late,
  Ere she sought her calm repose,
Pressed I, at the garden gate,
  Lips as sensuous as a rose.

Oh, the fancies which I reared!
  Built the future broad and fair—
Never once a flaw appeared
  In my castle in the air!

So, like leaves upon a stream,
  All the happy days went by
Then another came between,
  And we parted—she and I.

Here he read to her of May—
Whispered blithely in her ear:
Here she walked the pebbled way—
Sang the songs I loved to hear.

Though we smile at all love care,
Oft its memories ne'er depart;
So my castle in the air
Is in ruins round my heart.

This was a prophet's palimpsest, from whence
I drew the meaning of my cousin's words,
Which circled them—but late a Gyges ring.
Now I remembered how six years ago,
I read and walked with Dora in the lawn,
When Vivian, maddened by some jealous dread,
Had left her rashly, thinking me her choice.
So looking up, and comprehending all,
I saw their glances meet as lips.

A CAVE ECHO.

I come o'er sandhill and o'er wave,
  A whisper of the giant deep,
To echo down this granite cave,
  And find herein a charmèd sleep.
I break the silence far around,
  Which woos with weird Circean sway,
Though but the frightened shadow-sound,
  Of some sea-murmur passed away.
I sigh through glooms of stalactite—
  Circinal ferns I tremble by,
Till, set with light, the happy night
  Rolls star-capped billows up the sky.

I faint in savors of the spring:
  The cinque-drops i' the cowslips' breast,
And larks which "tirra lirra" sing,

All, all do tempt me back to rest.
I touched the silver coifs of waves,
And on the shore the fronded moss,
But here in gleamy, garnet caves,
Lo! all my gain doth end with loss.
I fly athwart the rocks, and flee
In jasper grottos dashed with stain,
Till unto me, the moon-led sea
Puts out its white spray-arms again.

A sweet mermaiden broke my rest,
Down where the coral halls are found;
She pressed me to her heaving breast,
And called me fairest rose of sound;
I stole away the while she slept—
I kissed her lips and stole away;
She did not dream that, while she slept,
Her rose would go to seek the May.
The downy foam, in folded mist,

Lay on her bosom, snow on snow ;
She little wist that as I kissed
I saw the crimson beads below.

I sailed the wrought asbestos floor,
Beneath the ceiling diamond-starred,
And all the castle wandered o'er,
Apast the drowsy merman guard.
I saw the mimic donjon-keep:
A rain of restless splendor gloom:
The spiky coral blushing deep;
And scallop censers burn perfume.
A dragon's gorge a fountain poured,
While white as snow-drop broke the spray ;
And when it lowered, a chanson soared,
And died in echoes far away.

Elna, my Elna, as the wind
Sways the sweet blossom pendant from a rock,
So all my heart doth sway before thy soul.

Elna, my Elna, as at dawn
The songs of unknown birds rise from the copse,
So nameless feelings rise before thine eyes.

The vine-fringed river spoke of thee:
The caves in lonely dimness asked of thee:
All things worship thee, Elna, my Elna.

O, I have loved thee more than life!
And as the glimmering stars are lost in morn,
So am I lost in thee, Elna, my Elna.

But naught the amber castle kept,
 Was half so dear as mermaid mine;
I could but watch her as she slept
 Upon the damasked berylline.
The finny half below her waist,
 In golden scales flashed up a charm;
And o'er her floating hair was placed,
 Tiara-sweet, a snowy arm.

Crowned with a ruby star, she seemed
  Like twilight mingling day and dusk;
And while she dreamed, the urn-lamp
    gleamed
  Through porphyry chambers rich with
    musk.

I kissed the mermaid once again—
  I passed where meads of sea-grass wave;
And, sighing as I left the main,
  I came to sleep within this cave.
Like joyous days which flit along—
  Those happy moments life doth crown,
Each echo seems a step of song,
  To depths of silence leading down.
My inessential being wanes;
  I falter as I murmur through
These dusky lanes of onyx stains—
  I faint—I die—a long adieu.

CLEON AT OROPOS.

CLEON the poet, famed throughout all Greece,
Mused o'er his tablets, in the palace hall.
And high the clear voice of a timbrel rose,
Delirious with rapture, half of pain.
Here Rhodope in marble, crowned with bays,
Supine, beside a pyramid of shade,
Swooned with white peace. And from his
carven niche,
Poising a flame-barbed spear, a warrior leaned
And battled with the shadows. Then to this,
Or of such import, shaped the restless thought:

My epos on these leaves of gold,
  Through which some depthless meanings gleam,
'Mid wordy petals fold on fold,
  Is crude beside my perfect dream.
For quick desire outstrips our deeds;
  And these but keep the ashes whole
  Of some strange passion of the soul,
E'en as a grate doth hold its gleeds.

But here is that which time may crown:
  Here burns the silver lamp of youth;
And great Minerva wanders down
  To prove that progress is a truth.
Here runs what idol-toil has gained
  To give this golden age its place;
  And here, eternity and space
Seem two vast circles, unexplained.

Here Venus, fanned with wooing gales,
  Which from her bright foam-palace flee,
Guiding her diamond pinnace, sails
  Along the calm, blue evening sea.
Nor hangs the suave drupe afar;
  Nor is the drused cliff hastened by:
  While sprent with glory looms the sky,
Scooped from some giant, sapphire star.

But men may say: Perforce he strives
  To light a torch of fame with straws.
Not so; but down our tidal lives,
  To point from wide effect to cause:
To make truth better understood;
  To throne fair freedom higher still;
  To show the broad results of will,
And prove that wrong must tend to good.

My words are weak: they do not hold
  The wine of thought I wished to pour:

It may be some are overbold;
  Well, they are mine, nor less, nor more.
But full fruition comes with time;
  For art shall cross the unknown sea,
  Precursor of the great To-Be,
And belt the world from clime to clime.

THE END.

www.ingramcontent.com/pod-product-compliance
Lightning Source LLC
LaVergne TN
LVHW021411110826
845150LV00007B/1880

* 9 7 8 1 4 2 5 5 1 1 2 0 3 *